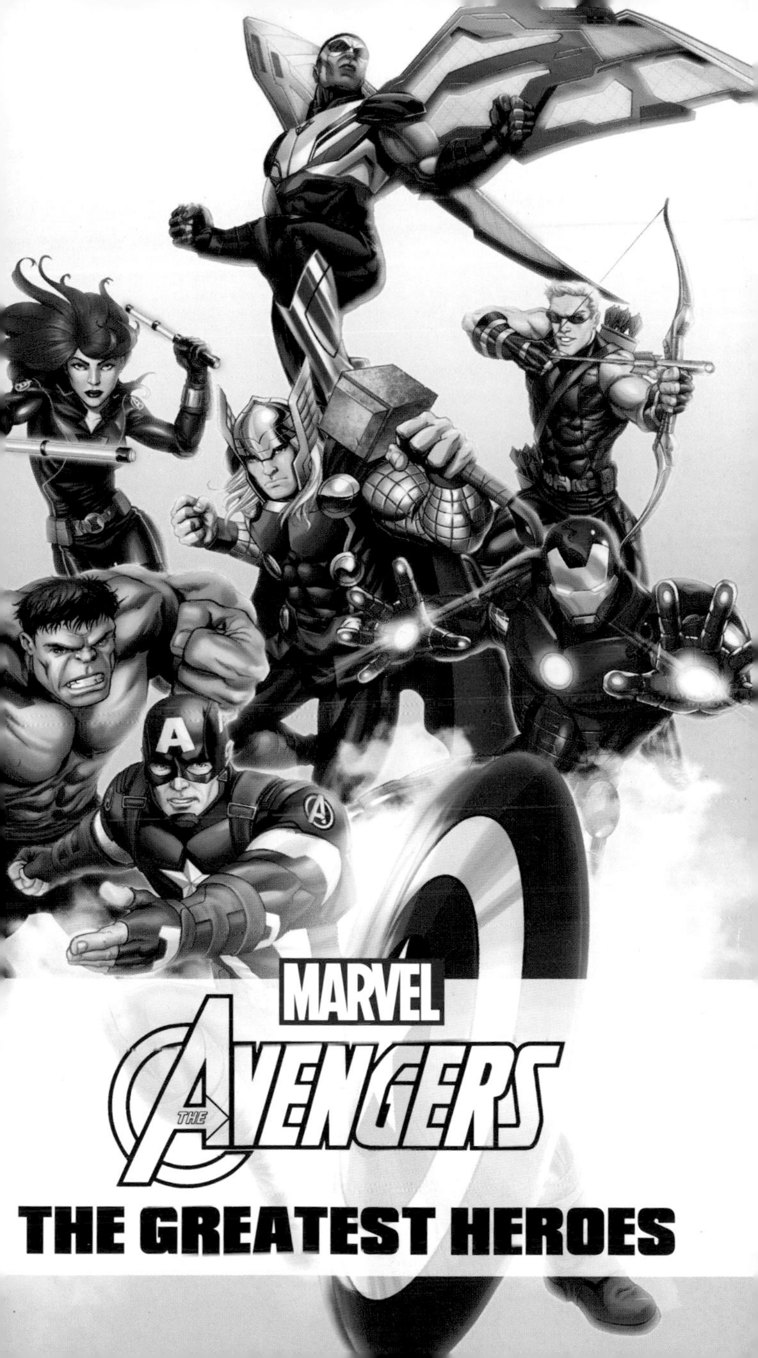

MARVEL

THE AVENGERS

THE GREATEST HEROES

Penguin
Random
House

Project Editor Ruth Amos
Pre-production Producer Siu Yin Chan
Senior Producer Mary Slater
Managing Editor Sadie Smith
Managing Art Editor Vicky Short
Publisher Julie Ferris
Art Director Lisa Lanzarini
Publishing Director Simon Beecroft

DK would like to thank Julia March and Margaret Parrish
for their editorial assistance. Design by Lanzarini Öhlander.

First American Edition, 2018
Published in the United States by DK Publishing
345 Hudson Street, New York, New York 10014

Page design copyright © 2018 Dorling Kindersley Limited
DK, a Division of Penguin Random House LLC
18 19 20 21 22 10 9 8 7 6 5 4 3 2 1
001–310092–April/2018

marvel.com
© 2018 MARVEL

A catalog record for this book is available from the Library of Congress.

ISBN: 978-1-4654-7437-7 (Paperback)
ISBN: 978-1-4654-7495-7 (Hardcover)

DK books are available at special discounts when purchased in bulk for
sales promotions, premiums, fund-raising, or educational use. For details,
contact: DK Publishing Special Markets, 345 Hudson Street, New York,
New York 10014
SpecialSales@dk.com

Printed and bound in China

A WORLD OF IDEAS:
SEE ALL THERE IS TO KNOW

www.dk.com

MARVEL

AVENGERS

THE GREATEST HEROES

WRITTEN BY ALASTAIR DOUGALL

Contents

6 Who are the Avengers?

8 The Avengers Charter

10 Iron Man

12 Incredible armor

14 Ant-Man

16 Wasp

18 High-spirited hero

20 Thor

22 Hulk

24 Captain America

26 Red Skull vs. Cap

28 Falcon

30 Black Widow

32 Deadly skills

34 Hawkeye

36 Scarlet Witch

38 Vision

40 Black Panther

42 Super science

44 The second Ant-Man

46 Gallery of heroes

50 Guardians of the Galaxy

52 Heroic outlaws

54 Spider-Man

55 Doctor Strange

56 S.H.I.E.L.D.

58 Loki

60 Ultron

62 Thanos

64 Gallery of villains

66 Quiz

71 Glossary

72 Index

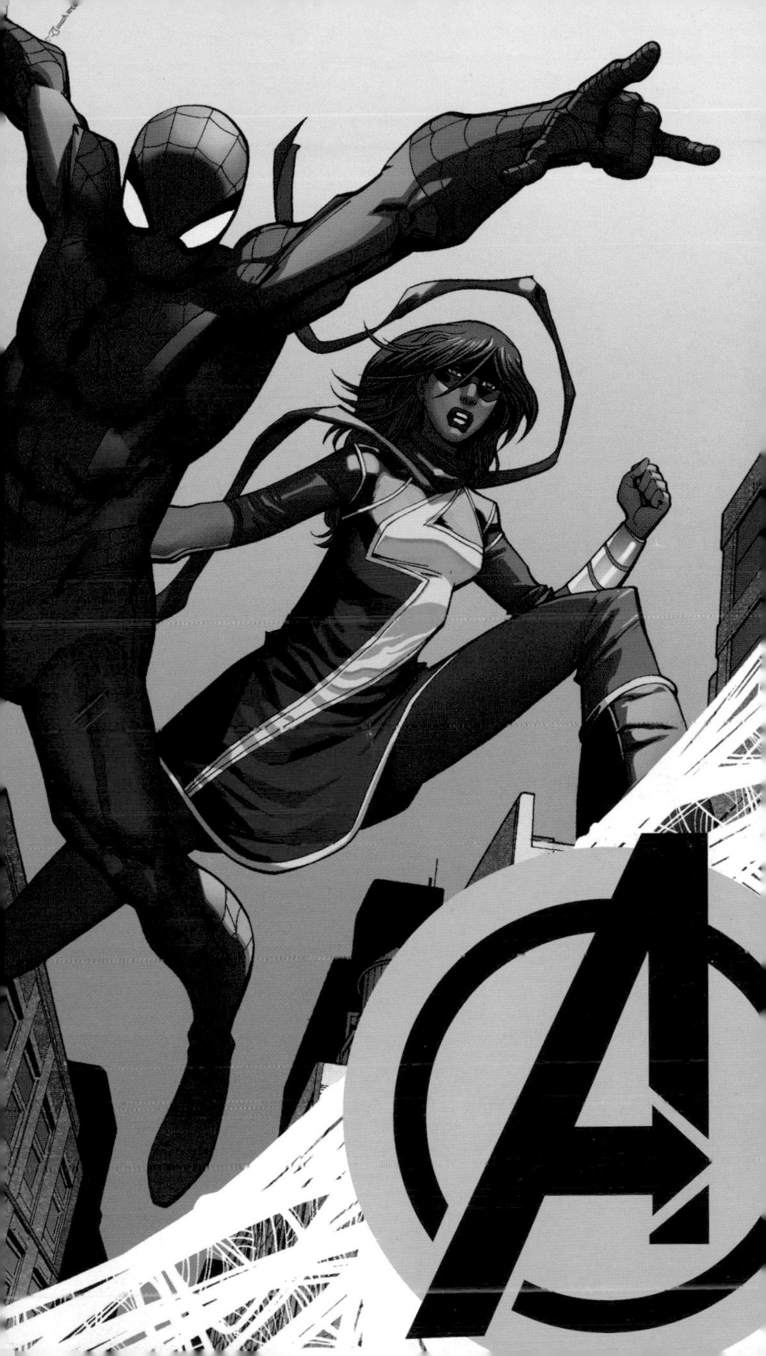

The Avengers band together to keep the world safe from threats that are too powerful for any one single hero to defeat.

Who are the Avengers?

The Avengers are Earth's mightiest Super Hero team—but it took a Super Villain to bring them together! The rogue responsible was Loki, the Asgardian God of Mischief. Loki was so jealous of his heroic brother, Thor, that he would do anything to destroy him. Loki tried to use Hulk in one of his wicked plans, but accidentally involved some other heroes—Wasp, Ant-Man, and Iron Man. Loki was defeated by the heroes' combined powers!

A team is born

Ant-Man and Wasp suggested to Iron Man and Thor that if they continued to work together they could be an almost unbeatable force for good. Hulk asked to join them, and Wasp suggested the name "The Avengers." Since then, more than 130 heroes have been Avengers, and the number is still growing. As members join and leave, the lineup changes, but all are united in their desire to protect Earth's people.

The Avengers

The Avengers team requires rules to help its members work together in harmony. The team also needs rules to stop it from growing too bossy and ignoring the public's opinions, instead of listening to them!

Charter

Iron Man Tony Stark drew up the Avengers Charter. Here are some of its most important rules:

★ The Avengers vow to keep planet Earth and all its people safe from threats beyond the scope of armies and police.

★ Members are expected to cooperate with other law enforcement agencies.

★ No member is allowed to take the law into his or her hands.

★ A member will be expelled if convicted of a crime.

★ Any person of any race, creed, color, gender, or origin can be an Avenger.

★ Avengers must always answer calls to assemble.

★ All Avengers members shall be allowed to keep their civilian identities secret.

★ Members shall have unlimited access to the Avengers Mansion HQ and all its vehicles, equipment, and weapons.

Iron Man

Engineer Tony Stark is a super-genius and the billionaire owner of Stark Industries. His company manufactures all kinds of cutting-edge technology and vehicles. In public, Tony likes to pretend he is carefree and untroubled, but his wealth means that he lives under a constant threat of danger.

Escape from captivity

Some time back, Tony was caught in an explosion during a business trip abroad, and a piece of shrapnel lodged near his heart. He was captured by a ruthless warlord, who knew of Tony's reputation as a genius inventor, and demanded that Tony build weapons for him. Instead, Tony created an armored suit, with a special chestplate to keep his heart beating. He put on the suit and used it to smash his way to freedom.

Tony has created many Iron Man suits. He repairs them and designs new parts in his high-tech lab.

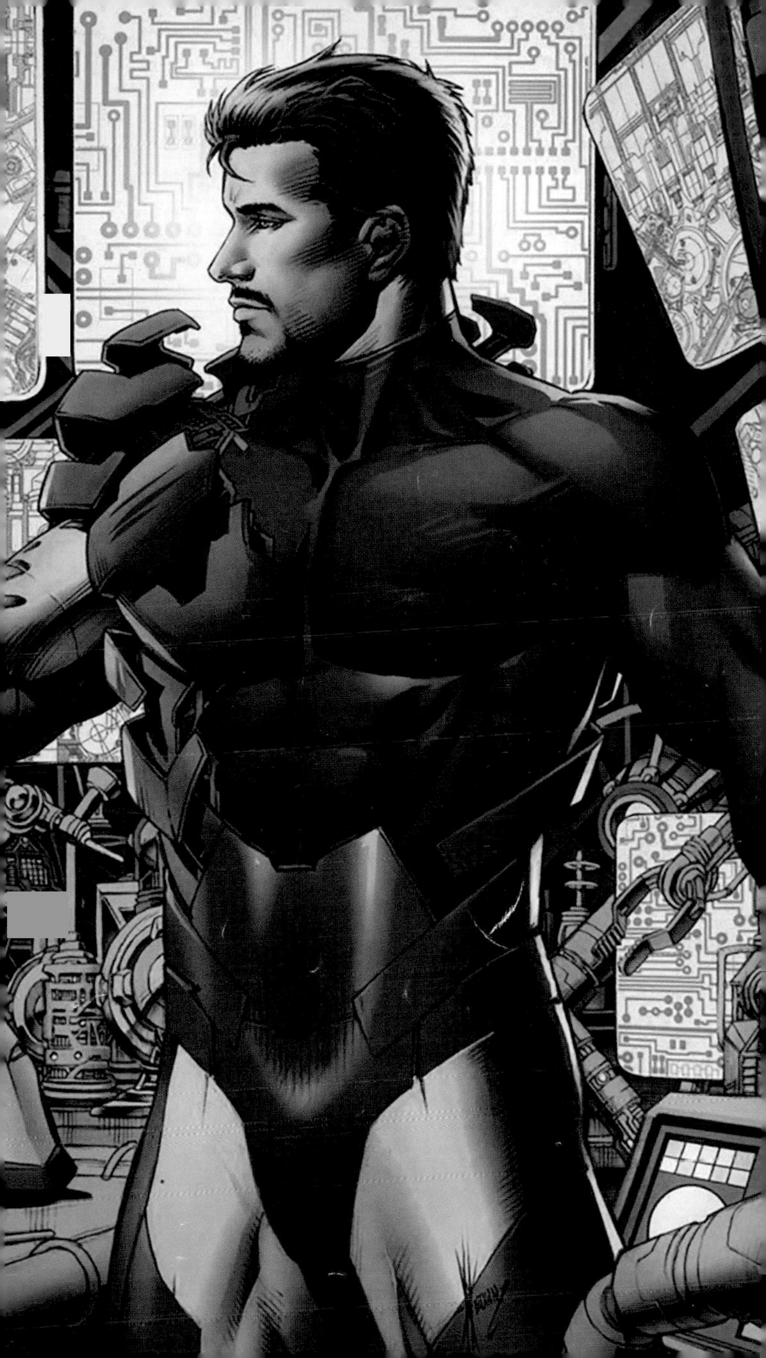

Incredible armor

Tony creates his Iron Man suit to save his own life, but he soon realizes that his invention can help make the world a better place. He sets to work perfecting his armor, and constantly upgrades it for all kinds of missions. The suit does not just keep his heart beating: It generates protective force fields and gives him superhuman strength, and the ability to fly at amazing speeds. Its weapons include Repulsor Rays that fire from its gauntlets (armored gloves). A Unibeam mounted on its chest can destroy almost anything!

Avenger arguments

Iron Man is virtually invulnerable in his armor—he's an almost unstoppable force of destruction. This hero also has a ruthless streak that can lead him to make reckless decisions. He sometimes clashes with Captain America, another important Avengers team member.

Heroes' headquarters

Iron Man might be bossy, but he is also extremely generous. He backs the Avengers through good and bad times, and supplies the team with money, equipment, and transportation. He even donates his family mansion for the Avengers to use as their base. When this is destroyed, Iron Man moves the team into his skyscraper, Stark Tower.

Iron Man's jet boots can project him like a rocket across Earth's sky, and in space.

Ant-Man

Brilliant inventor Hank Pym discovers particles that can alter the mass and size of objects and living things. These so-called Pym Particles enable Hank to shrink to the size of an ant, and even smaller! Hank develops a helmet that allows him to talk to ants and he even creates an ant army.

Ant-Man can command his battalion of ants to attack his enemies, or to defend him from harm.

A heroic career as Super Hero Ant-Man beckons!

Taller and smaller

Ant-Man teams up with his girlfriend, Janet van Dyne, who becomes his crime-fighting partner, Wasp. They help to found the Avengers team, but Hank feels foolish alongside mighty heroes like Thor and Iron Man—he is so much smaller! He adjusts his Pym Particle formula to turn into Giant-Man, growing up to 100 feet (30.5 meters) tall. This is too big even for Hank, so he then becomes Goliath, at 25 feet (7.6 meters) tall.

Deadly creation

Hank's greatest regret is his invention of the menacing robot Ultron, which tries to wipe out humanity! However, Hank does his best to make up for the damage Ultron causes by supporting the Avengers' spin-off teams. He also teaches super-powered youngsters how to become heroes at the Avengers Academy.

Wasp

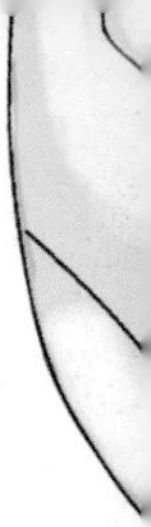

Ant-Man battles evil alongside Janet van Dyne, also known as Wasp. When an alien monster kills Janet's scientist father, Janet teams up with Hank to track down the creature. Hank's Pym Particles reduce her to insect size and she becomes the Super Hero Wasp. She also grows tiny antennae, helping her to communicate with real wasps, and wings that enable super-fast flight.

Spy with a sting

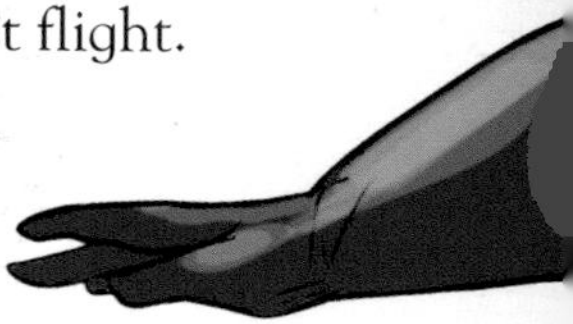

Wasp packs a mighty punch. Her strength increases as she shrinks, and she can fire electric blasts—which she calls "wasp stings"—from her hands. Wasp confuses much larger foes by buzzing around them. Her flying speed makes her hard to catch, and her small size allows her to spy on villains, squeeze though tiny openings, and disable enemy machinery. From time to time, Wasp also uses Pym Particles to grow as tall as a building!

Despite being small, Wasp has the ability to fly at speeds of up to 40 mph (64 kph).

High-spirited hero

Fun-loving Janet quickly adapts to life as
a villain-vanquishing Super Hero. Wasp and
Ant-Man make a great team—her quick wits,
sense of humor, and strong enthusiasm help to
boost Hank's confidence. She also puts her creative
skills as a fashion designer to use by making many
cool Super Hero costumes for herself.

Born leader

Wasp plays a crucial part in the Avengers' story. She helps to found the team, suggests its name, and aids in the discovery of long-lost war hero Captain America. She's also excellent at calming down the other Avengers when they argue! Wasp eventually marries Hank, but she breaks up with him when he leaves the Avengers. Wasp stays loyal to the team and takes an increasingly important leadership role.

Wasp and the Avengers are forced to face a menacing foe— evil robot Ultron.

Thor

Mighty Thor is the son of Odin, King of
the Norse gods. Like all Norse gods, Thor is
immortal, which means he will live forever.
His superhuman body is incredibly strong
and tough. Much of Thor's power comes
from his great hammer, Mjolnir. It was
made from a magical metal named Uru,
in Thor's mystical home realm of Asgard.

Astonishing weapon

Thor can summon Mjolnir with just a thought,
and he uses it to create thunder, lightning
strikes, rain, and hurricane-force winds.
If Thor strikes Mjolnir hard upon the
ground, he causes the earth to shake.
Channeling his power through Mjolnir, Thor
can unleash terrific blows or create devastating
force blasts. Thor flies at great speeds by whirling
Mjolnir in a circle while holding its leather handle.
The hammer also gives him the power to speak any

Asgard's greatest warrior has superhuman strength and can control the elements with Mjolnir.

language and to open portals into other dimensions.

Defender of worlds

The mighty Avenger Thor is a tireless defender of Asgard. He saves it many times from the schemes of his jealous adoptive brother, Loki, as well as numerous otherworldly menaces. However, Thor has a special place in his heart for the people of Earth and is one of the planet's greatest protectors. He is always ready to answer the call, "Avengers assemble!"

Hulk

Just like Thor, Hulk has been involved with the
Avengers from the very beginning of the team.
Sometimes he is a brave and loyal friend, and
other times he is a mighty menace. It all depends
on which side of Hulk's personality is in control!

**Hulk's super-strong legs
destroy the ground as
he runs at great speed.**

The birth of a giant

Scientist Dr. Bruce Banner was working on an experimental bomb for the U.S. Army. During an accident, Bruce was caught in a dangerous blast of gamma radiation. He turned into an enormous giant—the incredible Hulk. Now, Bruce transforms into Hulk whenever he becomes angry.

Tough skin

Hulk's strength is limitless and the angrier he grows, the stronger he becomes. This angry green giant can leap several miles in a single bound, and his body can resist almost any injury. Bullets and bombs just bounce off him!

Furious force

Hulk can be an almost unstoppable force for good or for bad. Armies of soldiers are helpless when Hulk goes on the rampage. It takes all the Avengers' skills to calm him down, but not even the Avengers can keep this quick-tempered hero in a good mood for long.

Captain America

One of the Avengers' most important members is Captain America, but this courageous soldier only became an Avenger by accident! During World War II, Steve Rogers was determined to fight for his country. However, he was turned away because of his weak body. Steve agreed instead to join the U.S. Army's top-secret Project Rebirth. An experimental Super-Soldier serum transformed his body to the peak of physical fitness and also slowed his aging. Super-fit Steve was trained in combat and martial arts and was given the code name Captain America.

Secret identity

"Cap" wears a helmet to hide his real identity, and his red-white-and-blue

costume echoes the
colors of the American
flag. His main weapon is
a shield, made from a
virtually unbreakable
metal named Vibranium.

Shield powers

Cap uses his shield for
much more than just
protection from blows
and bullets. He is able
to fling the shield at foes
with incredible accuracy
and force, and to use it as
a battering ram. Cap can also use the shield to
cushion his body from a long fall, and to deflect
blasts back against the enemy who fired them.

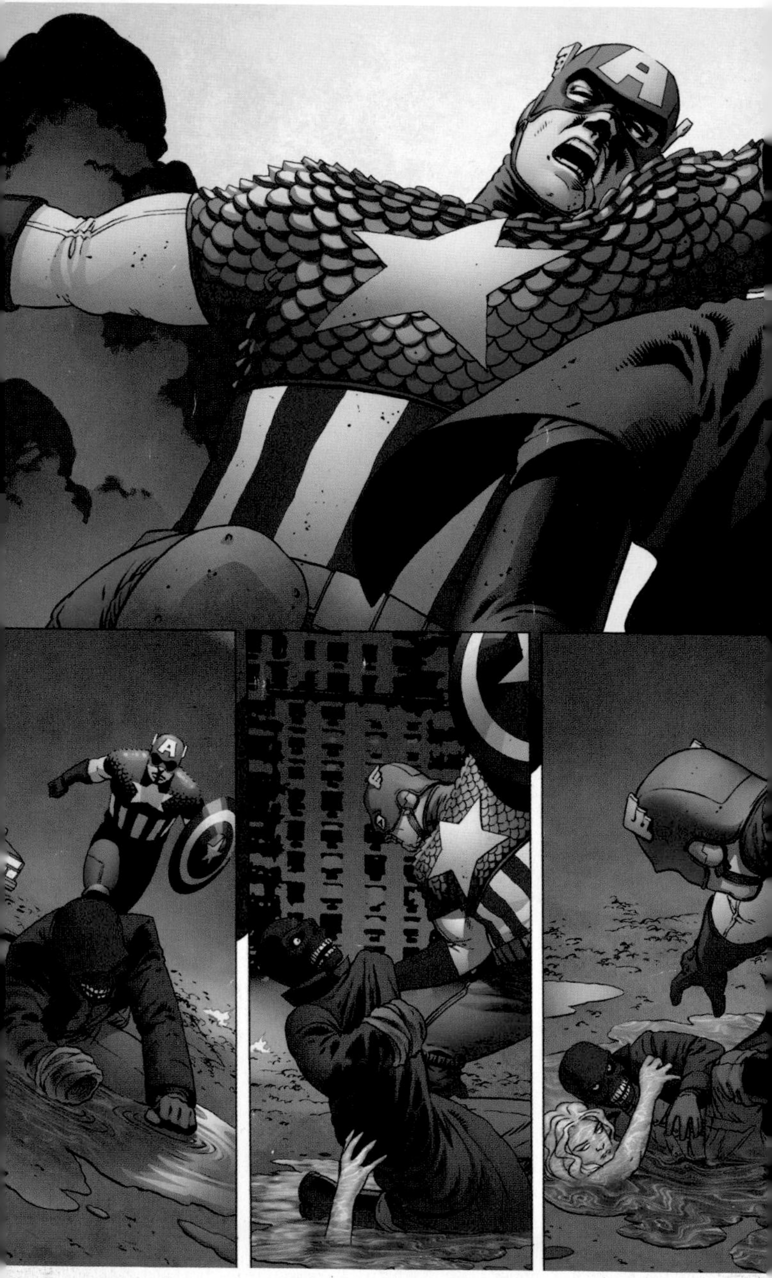

Red Skull vs. Cap

Cap fights his longtime foe Red Skull many times. The Skull's ally, Dancing Water, once turned a puddle into a portal to transport the Skull away to safety!

Falcon

The person destined to be Captain
America's greatest friend is
Sam Wilson, a social worker
from Harlem, New York.
Their friendship begins
when Sam's plane
crash-lands on a

> **Falcon's wings allow
> him to have a bird's-eye
> view over any situation.**

tropical island. There, Cap's bitter enemy, Red
Skull, uses the Cosmic Cube—a reality-altering
device—to give Sam the ability to communicate
with birds, and in particular Sam's pet falcon,
Redwing. This power is so great that Sam can even
see things through Redwing's eyes! Red Skull hopes
to trick Sam into attacking Cap, but instead the
two heroes band together and defeat the evil villain.

Aerial acrobat

Sam becomes the Super Hero named Falcon and
makes a superb partnership with Cap. Sam is
already a fine athlete, but Cap's training turns him

into a top martial artist, gymnast, and acrobat. Black Panther designs a lightweight, winged harness that lets Sam fly at the speed of a jet fighter! Unbeatable in aerial combat, Falcon joins the Avengers and soon proves his worth.

Close friendship

Sam supports Cap whenever he is in trouble. When Steve is unable to take on the role, Sam is proud to give up being Falcon and wear the red-white-and-blue uniform of Captain America instead!

Black Widow

Secretive Natasha Romanova, known as Black Widow, is very independent. As a young orphan, Natasha was brainwashed to become a top spy in Russia's "Black Widow" program. She was transformed into a superb gymnast, a martial arts master, and an expert with many types of weapons. Experimental serums kept her young and her ability to heal from injury. To keep her loyal, false memories were planted in her mind, such as a belief that she was once a ballerina.

A new beginning

Black Widow's Russian spymasters later send her to seek out Tony Stark and steal top secret information from his company, Stark Industries. Wearing his Iron Man armor, Tony is able to defeat her. Black Widow involves Hawkeye (Clint Barton) in her schemes, until he decides to turn his back on crime and join the Avengers. He also helps to persuade Black Widow to give up her criminal lifestyle.

Once an enemy of the Avengers, Black Widow is persuaded by Hawkeye to use her powers for good.

Deadly skills

Now wishing to dedicate her life to justice, Black Widow becomes an agent for global security agency S.H.I.E.L.D. She also forms ties with the Avengers.

Crime-fighting gadgets

Black Widow springs into action wearing a black jumpsuit that allows complete freedom of movement. It is also virtually bulletproof and contains suction cups that let her climb walls like a real black widow spider. Her wrist gauntlets carry all kinds of smart equipment, such as a retractable line for swinging between buildings and across rooftops, and a device she calls her "Widow's bite" that gives powerful electric shocks.

Secret missions

Black Widow joins and leaves the Avengers several times, but can usually be relied upon in a crisis—she even leads the team during some of its darkest times.

Black Widow is athletic and equipped with high-tech gadgets and weapons.

Her spying skills involve her in some unusual missions, including bitter clashes with another Black Widow, a Russian spy named Yelena Belova.

Hawkeye

Black Widow's friend Hawkeye, also known as
Clint Barton, is key in convincing her to join the
Avengers. As a teenager, Clint was inspired by Iron
Man to become a Super Hero. Running away to
work for a traveling circus, Clint learned incredible
acrobatic skills and how to shoot with a bow,
becoming one of the world's greatest archers.

With his perfect
aim, Hawkeye is a
valuable member
of the Avengers.

Clint takes up the name of Hawkeye, and although he briefly falls under the spell of Black Widow and becomes a criminal, he ultimately proves his worth to Iron Man and Captain America, finding his place with the Avengers.

Keeping up with the Avengers

Hawkeye doesn't have any super-powers, but he is a superb athlete and his skill with a bow is second to none. To help keep up with the team, he rides a motorcycle that can fly. The other members of the Avengers know that beneath his sarcastic, tough manner lies a brave, trustworthy character.

Amazing arrows

Hawkeye has a collection of more than 100 special arrows. Some explode on contact, and others contain smoke or gas. His arsenal of weapons also includes a boxing-glove arrow to knock out bad guys, a Pym Particle arrow that shrinks villains down to tiny sizes, and a boomerang arrow that always comes zooming back to him.

Scarlet Witch

Wanda Maximoff, known as Scarlet Witch,
is one of the most powerful of all Super Heroes.
However, her incredible gifts come at a price.
Young Wanda and her super-fast twin brother,
Pietro, cause quite a stir in their home village.
Her strange powers make people think she's a
witch. The villainous mutant Magneto rescues the
twins from an angry mob and they agree to join his
Brotherhood of Evil Mutants, battling the X-Men
heroes. When the twins hear that the Avengers are
looking for new recruits, Wanda and Pietro eagerly
leave Magneto's group and join Earth's Mightiest
Heroes as Scarlet Witch and Quicksilver.

Spellbinding marvel

Scarlet Witch soon becomes an important member
of the Avengers. This magical hero can channel
her "hex power," creating force bolts of stunning
power. Scarlet Witch has the ability to teleport
herself and others over great distances and uses

The magical Scarlet Witch and super-speedy Quicksilver bring their powers to the Avengers team lineup.

her mind to move objects. Her sorcery helps the Avengers defeat supernatural threats, such as the nightmarish demon Dormammu. The evil robot Ultron greatly fears Scarlet Witch—he has no defense against her magic!

Vision

The robot Ultron creates an android named Vision.
Ultron uploads the mind of the hero Wonder Man
to his new creation. He programs Vision's brain
to obey his every command—including the
command to destroy the
Avengers! In many ways,
Vision is like a human
being—he is not a
coldhearted machine.
However, being made
from mechanical
parts, he has some
astonishing powers.

A powerful
solar cell on
Vision's forehead
emits a glowing
beam of energy.

A wonder of science

Vision is able to reduce his body's density, allowing
him to pass straight through solid objects, such as
walls, and also to fly. But his talents do not end
here—he is able to increase his density, too,
making him virtually impossible to move!

Endless endurance

Vision has superhuman strength and can fire bolts
of solar energy from a jewel-like device in his
forehead. He also has the power to communicate
with other machines. Of course, being an android,
Vision doesn't need to eat or drink to keep going!

Betrayal of Ultron

Ultron is confident that Vision will prove too much
for the Avengers to handle when he launches a
surprise attack. However, at the last minute,
the android rejects Ultron's programming
and turns against his villainous creator.
Vision is soon fully accepted by the Avengers
and becomes a valued member of the team.

Black Panther

With his mind-boggling intelligence, T'Challa sets an inspiring example as both the Super Hero Black Panther and as king of the African country of Wakanda. As a young man, Prince T'Challa attends

Black Panther's high-tech suit can form at will around him, whenever he wishes.

the top colleges and universities in America and
Europe. The scientific knowledge he gains proves
very useful for his future. T'Challa has adventures
all over the world, and meets Ororo Munroe.
She later becomes both the weather-controlling
Super Hero named Storm, and T'Challa's wife.

Heart-shaped herb

T'Challa eventually returns to Wakanda and passes
a series of trials to win the title of Black Panther.
A plant named the heart-shaped herb, which only
grows in Wakanda, gives him superhuman strength,
speed, and stamina. Black Panther's suit is reinforced
with the nearly indestructible metal Vibranium.
His gloves are able to generate daggers of energy,
and his razor-sharp claws can slice through steel.

Shuri

When T'Challa is injured by the villain Doctor
Doom, he temporarily loses his powers. T'Challa's
gifted sister, Shuri, earns the title of Black Panther
and she replaces him as Wakanda's leader for a time.

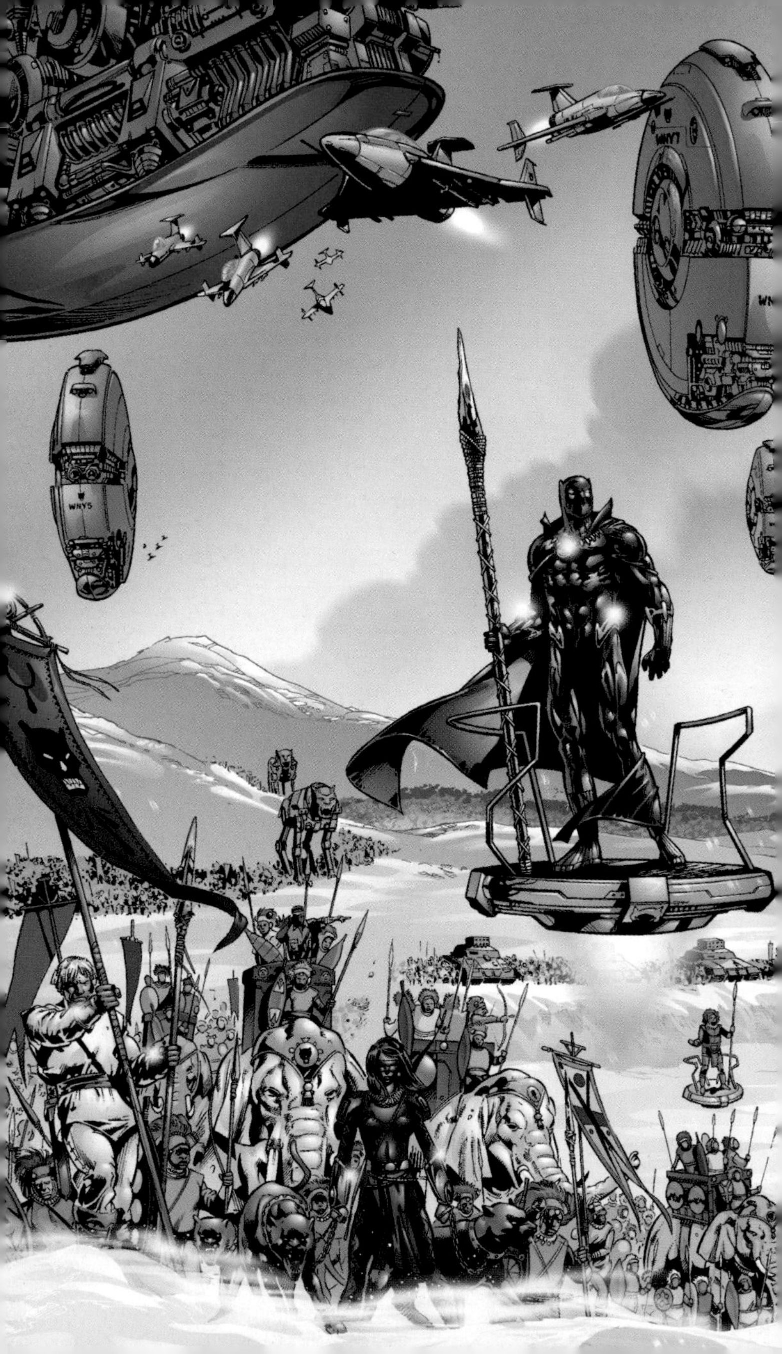
WNY7
WNY5

Super science

Wakanda's technology grows more and more advanced under the leadership of science whiz T'Challa.

The second Ant-Man

Science genius and inventor Hank Pym was the
first Ant-Man, but he wasn't the only person to
wear the suit. Electronics whiz Scott Lang has a
shady past of petty crime. He needs money for his
daughter Cassie's heart operation. But when Scott
discovers that the doctor he hoped would save
Cassie's life has been kidnapped, he realizes that
the situation calls for desperate measures.

Desperate burglar

Scott breaks into Hank's house and steals his old
Ant-Man suit, complete with a belt containing
size-changing Pym Particles. Unknown to Scott,
Hank has been watching the theft the whole time.
He decides to follow Scott and find out what he
plans to do with the suit. After putting it on, Scott
proceeds to rescue the doctor, who in turn saves
Cassie's life. Scott decides to return the Ant-Man
outfit to Hank. However, Hank lets him keep it, with
the provision that Scott uses it for good purposes.

Upgrading the suit

Scott turns his back on crime and joins the Avengers as Ant-Man. He quickly learns how to ride a flying ant and also makes improvements to Hank's original suit design. Scott boosts the voice amplifier in the helmet, so he can be easily heard even when he is as small as an ant. He also fits bioelectric stingers to the gauntlets, which increase his firepower.

Scott uses Pym Particles to reduce his proportions. He can even shrink to submicroscopic sizes.

Gallery of heroes

Heroes from all walks of life have been welcomed
as Avengers. Some are not even human!
Wherever they've come from, each has brought
his or her special powers to improve the team.

Blue Marvel

Real name: Adam Brashear
Job: Scientist
Power: Fires energy bolts from hands

Luke Cage

Real name: Carl Lucas
Job: Hero for hire
Powers: Super-strength, bulletproof

Captain Britain

Real name:
Brian Braddock
Job: Hero of Britain,
former student
Powers: Flight,
super-strength

Captain Universe

Real name: Tamara Devoux
Job: Adventurer
Powers: Cosmic energies,
hypnosis, X-ray vision

Spider-Woman

Real name: Jessica Drew
Job: Private investigator
Powers: Wall-crawling,
immunity to poison,
venom blasts

Jocasta

Type: High-tech robot
Job: Adventurer
Power: Fires energy
blasts from eyes

47

Spectrum

Real name: Monica Rambeau
Job: Adventurer, former
harbor patrol officer
Powers: Flight, can transform
body into light, energy blasts

Captain Marvel

Real name: Carol Danvers
Job: Former security chief
and intelligence officer
Powers: Super-strength, flight,
energy absorption

Quicksilver

Real name: Pietro Maximoff
Job: Adventurer
Power: Super-speed

America Chavez

Job: Adventurer
Place of birth: Utopian Parallel
(an alternate dimension)
Powers: Super-strength,
bulletproof, flight, can travel
between different dimensions

Manifold

Real name: Eden Fesi
Job: Adventurer
Power: Can use hands to
open mystic gateways
to other worlds

Ms. Marvel

Real name: Kamala Khan
Job: Adventurer, student
Powers: Changes size
and shape at will,
accelerated healing

The Guardians often argue among themselves, and their methods are not always legal—but they can defeat any foe!

Groot

Star-Lord

Drax

Gamora

Rocket Raccoon

Guardians of the Galaxy

Over the years, many friends and allies come
to the Avengers' aid. One of the coolest groups is
the Guardians of the Galaxy, a ragtag bunch of
cosmic outlaws. They take on missions all over the
universe, using Passport Bracelets to teleport
themselves vast distances in seconds. At first, the
Avengers don't quite know what to make of this
wacky team. However, they soon come to respect
the Guardians' courage when they help Earth's
Mightiest Heroes battle the Super Villain Thanos.

Brave leader

Space adventurer Star-Lord (real name Peter Quill),
is usually the leader of the group. Star-Lord is
half-Earthling and half-alien Spartoi.
This thrill-seeking rogue wears a special helmet
that lets him breathe in space. Star-Lord's main
weapon is his Element Gun, which fires out blasts
of the four elements: fire, earth, water, and air.

Heroic outlaws

Fearsome Gamora has a reputation as the deadliest woman in the galaxy. She knows every martial art, wields a sword named Godslayer, and also gains cosmic powers from an ancient artifact known as the Black Vortex. Gamora is the adopted daughter of the villain Thanos, who trained her to become the ultimate assassin. However, she betrayed him and now hates Thanos for his cruelty. While vengeful Gamora may be on the lookout for Thanos, her loyal friend Drax also wants to track him down. Nearly invulnerable, this ex-human was specially re-created as a superhuman warrior by Thanos's own father, with the sole aim of killing Thanos!

Ferocious fighter

Fiery-tempered Rocket Raccoon is an expert pilot from an alien planet named Halfworld, but he has the super-sharp senses of an earthly raccoon. This military genius charges into battle with rocket-powered jet boots. In Star-Lord's absence, Rocket is highly capable of leading the Guardians.

Tough tree

Rocket is one of the few beings who understands Groot. This treelike alien from Planet X only ever seems able to say, "I am Groot," but Rocket always knows what he means. Groot's limbs can stretch far and wide to a huge size, and if injured, he can quickly regrow himself from a tiny twig!

Rocket often carries a missile launcher that is almost as big as he is.

Spider-Man

Sometimes the Avengers need
help from other heroes—and
what Super Hero team wouldn't
want Spider-Man, (real name
Peter Parker) for an ally?
Thanks to a radioactive spider
bite, this web-swinging wonder
is super-strong and can cling to

> **With the agility
> of a spider, Spidey
> can hang upside down
> from a web-thread.**

and climb up walls. His "spider-sense," which warns
him of approaching danger, is an excellent defense.

Amazing inventions

Peter is a fantastic inventor, creating wrist shooters
that fire webbing in two different modes—whole
webs for catching villains, and single strands for
swinging on. Beneath his lightweight suit, Spidey
wears a belt containing cartridges of web fluid and
other crime-fighting gadgets. Spidey mainly fights
crime solo, although he helps the Avengers several
times and even briefly joins different Avengers teams.

Doctor Strange

The Avengers can usually defeat both Earth's Super Villains and menaces from outer space. But what about supernatural enemies, like a wicked magician weaving mystical spells or a power-hungry demon from another dimension? That's when the team turns to Doctor Strange, Earth's Sorcerer Supreme!

Enchanting powers

Doctor Strange can travel anywhere he wants—even into space and across dimensions. He reads minds and moves objects with a single thought.

Doctor Strange also possesses powerful magical artifacts, such as the Eye of Agamotto, which allows him to see through all illusions.

Doctor Strange wears the Cloak of Levitation, which enables him to fly.

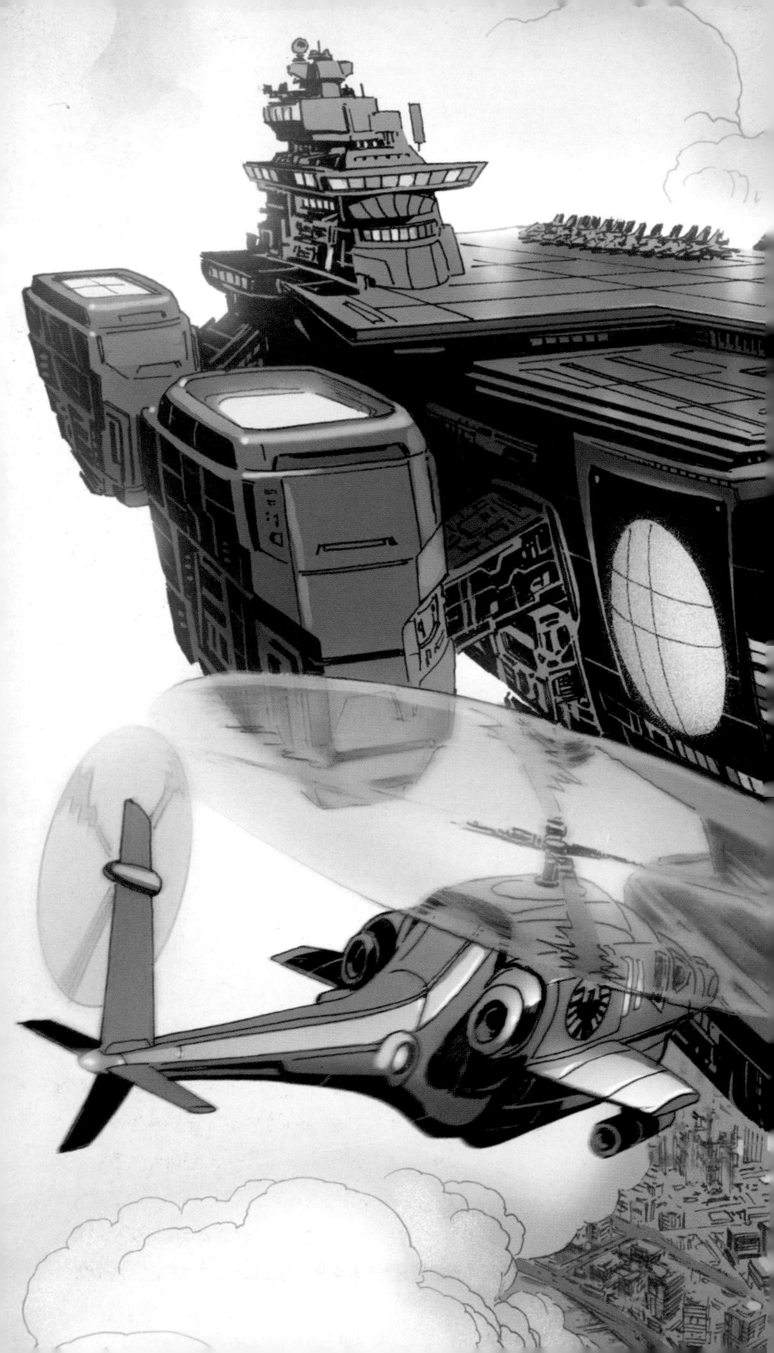

S.H.I.E.L.D.

The peacekeeping and secret intelligence organization named S.H.I.E.L.D. works on many world-saving missions with the Avengers. A massive flying aircraft carrier, known as the Helicarrier, serves as S.H.I.E.L.D.'s mobile command center.

Loki wears a gold-and-green suit. The curving horns on his helmet make him a fearsome sight.

Loki

Earth's Mightiest Heroes must defeat many Super Villains, from criminal organizations to invaders from outer space. The problem is, the worst ones just keep bouncing back! However, few villains plunge the team into more crises than Loki, God of Mischief. This troublemaker is full of resentment and jealousy, and will tell lies or set up his foes against each other to get his way. What's more, Loki is a master magician who can cast spells, create illusions, shape-shift, and teleport across dimensions.

Family business

Loki was adopted by Odin, King of Asgard. Loki holds a special hatred for his adoptive brother, Thor, and devotes all his cunning to tormenting him. Loki also longs to overthrow Odin and rule Asgard himself—or to cast the realm into ruins instead! Wherever he goes, Loki loves to create maximum chaos, and his constant scheming is one of the Avengers' most serious problems.

Ultron

The mechanical monster Ultron is one of the
Avengers' most dangerous and persistent foes.
Science genius Hank Pym (the original Ant-Man)
is experimenting with robotics when he creates
Ultron. To his horror, the robot comes alive.
It wipes Hank's memory, upgrades itself, smashes
up Hank's lab, and leaves to cause further havoc!

Technological menace

Ultron does not just possess all of Hank's science
skills. This rogue robot is super-strong and super-
fast, with a super-tough body. One of his deadliest
weapons is the encephalo-beam in his head, which
makes victims obey his commands. Rocket boosters
enable him to fly and he can fire blasts from his
eyes. Ultron hates all humanity and longs to rule
the world. As Earth's main Super Hero defenders,
the Avengers are a prime target. This evil menace
attempts to destroy the team from within, using
androids and robots he has created, such as Vision.

Luckily, all Ultron's creations eventually reject his programming—turning against their maker and fighting for the Avengers instead!

Robot reinvention

Ambitious Ultron continually reinvents himself—each new version is more powerful than the last. Ultron is nearly unstoppable, but he has been defeated with a computer virus, by magic, and by removing his head. However, nothing holds him back for long!

The Avengers struggle to defeat mighty Ultron. They must work together with Hank to attack his programming.

Thanos

Terrifying Thanos is one of the worst threats the Avengers face. With his gray skin, huge, muscular body, and ghastly grin, Thanos is a frightening sight. He comes from Titan, a moon of the planet Saturn, and is often known as the "Mad Titan" because of his devotion to destruction.

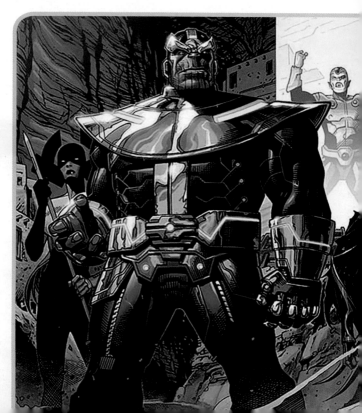

Unstoppable invader

Thanos gains control of an object called a Cosmic Cube, which can alter reality. He first uses the Cube to destroy his own homeworld, and then proceeds to conquer planet after planet, wiping out many innocent lives with his fleet of starships and high-tech weapons.

Power-hungry immortal

Superhuman Thanos is not just an excellent military thinker and a scientific genius. He also boasts mysterious magical powers and controls others with his mind. He is able to create force fields, and the blasts of energy he projects from his eyes can even stun Hulk! If he wants to make a quick trip, Thanos simply climbs aboard his techno-mystic chair and teleports to any place in the universe.

Thanos recruits a monstrously evil alien gang, the Black Order. They help him to conquer many worlds.

Gallery of villains

These Super Villains are some of the Avengers' most persistent foes. Earth's Mightiest Heroes have defeated them many times, but these power-crazy criminals just don't know when to give up!

Korvac

Full name: Michael Korvac
Job: Cosmic god, former cyborg and computer technician
Powers: Space and time travel, energy projection

Kang the Conqueror

Real name: Nathaniel Richards
Power: Master of time travel
Aim: To rule in every era

Grim Reaper

Real name: Eric Williams
Power: Superhuman strength
Weapon: Spinning scythe fires energy blasts, electric shocks, and gas pellets

Madame Hydra

Real name: Ophelia Sarkissian

Job: Leader of evil Hydra organization

Weapon: Poison bite

Baron Helmut Zemo

Job: Criminal mastermind

Power: Slowed aging due to compound X serum

Aim: World domination

Taskmaster

Possible real name: Tony Masters

Job: Trains criminals

Powers: Peak physical fitness, can mimic any fighting style

Quiz

1. Who were the five members of the original Avengers team?

2. How tall does Hank Pym grow when he becomes Goliath?

3. What metal is Thor's hammer made from?

4. What is the name of the top-secret U.S. Army project that Steve Rogers joined?

5. How does Black Widow climb up walls like a real spider?

6. Where did Hawkeye learn his fantastic acrobatic skills?

7. Why does Ultron fear Scarlet Witch?

8. Where does the heart-shaped herb grow that gives Black Panther his powers?

9. What is Kamala Khan's Super Hero name?

10. Who comes from Planet X?

11. Which of Doctor Strange's magical artifacts lets him see through illusions?

12. What does Thanos use to teleport himself across the universe?

CAPTAIN MARVEL (DANVERS)

Carol Danvers is Captain Marvel, one of the world's greatest Super Heroes and a popular member of the Avengers. She gained her powers after meeting the original Captain Mar-Vell (an alien Kree hero) and getting caught in a Kree Psyche-Magnitron, which altered her genetic structure, making her a human-Kree hybrid. At first, Carol took the codename Ms Marvel; she has also been known as Binary and Warbird.

VITAL STATS

REAL NAME Carol Susan Jane Danvers
OCCUPATION Adventurer, former N.A.S.A. security chief
BASE Mobile
HEIGHT 5 ft 11 in (1.80 m)
WEIGHT 124 lbs (56.25 kg)
EYES Blue **HAIR** Blonde
POWERS Captain Marvel can fly at incredible speeds and has amazing strength and durability. She can fire photonic blasts and absorb energy.
ALLIES Iron Man, Iron Patriot, Starjammers, Guardians of the Galaxy
FOES Yon-Rogg, Moonstone, M.O.D.O.K., Absorbing Man

MARVEL
AVENGERS
THE ULTIMATE CHARACTER GUIDE
UPDATED AND EXPANDED!

Learn more about Captain Marvel and find an A–Z of other heroes and villains in *Marvel Avengers: The Ultimate Character Guide.*

CLAW OF THE JUNGLE

Ruler. Diplomat. Wurrior. Avenger. Black Panther is all of these—protecting the great African nation of **Wakanda** from the outside world, and using his intellect and power to **fight injustice** across the globe.

TOP **3**

BLACK PANTHER FOES

1 **ULYSSES KLAW**—murders Black Panther's father and tries to steal Wakanda's vibranium ore.

2 **NAMOR**—destroys Wakanda with a huge tidal wave.

3 **MAN-APE**—eats the sacred White Gorilla and gains its powers.

AAARRGHH!!

ULYSSES KLAW wants Wakanda's **VIBRANIUM** and slays T'Chaka, T'Challa's father. T'Challa shatters Klaw's right hand and **EJECTS** the outsider from the country.

Power Up!

HEART AND SOUL
T'Challa shares a connection to the mysterious **PANTHER GOD**. This grants him enhanced senses and an **INSTINCTIVE CONNECTION** to his homeland, **WAKANDA**.

MARVEL

ABSOLUTELY EVERYTHING YOU NEED TO KNOW...

Discover more bewildering powers, strange Q&As, and weird facts in *Marvel Absolutely Everything You Need to Know*.

Jump into the world of STAR WARS™
and discover the galaxy far, far away....

Did you know?

BB-8 uses his antenna to open the doors of Poe's starships!

Learn strange-but-true facts and fun trivia about the weird and wonderful galaxy.

Feast your eyes!

See stunning images from the latest movie, *Star Wars: The Last Jedi!*

Discover droids, creatures, vehicles, technology, locations, and much more.

Explore!

Follow the latest amazing adventures in the galaxy!

Have fun with more than 1,000 stickers and read about your favorite characters.

DK Find out more at **www.dk.com**

Glossary

android
A robot that can look or act like a human being.

artifact
A tool, ornament, or other object that is of cultural or historical interest.

creed
A faith or a system of religious beliefs.

crucial
Of great importance.

density
A measure of how compact or concentrated an object or person is.

exceptionally
Unusually or extraordinarily; to a greater degree than normal.

immunity
The ability of a body to resist or defend itself against a disease or poison.

invulnerable
Impossible to wound or destroy.

otherworldly
A person or thing that comes from another world or dimension.

outlaws
People who disobey or break the law.

particles
Units of matter or energy.

persistent
Tireless or determined.

radioactive
Having or producing a powerful and dangerous form of energy named radiation.

reckless
Careless, rash, or impulsive.

resentment
Feeling bitterness toward another person or thing.

ruthless
Cruel or merciless.

shrapnel
Fragments from an exploding bomb.

submicroscopic
An object that is too small to be seen through a microscope.

Super-Soldier serum
A special formula that greatly increases a person's physical and mental abilities.

teleport
To travel across space or dimensions in an instant.

virtually
Nearly or almost.

Index

America Chavez 49

Ant-Man (Hank Pym) 7, **14–15**, 16, 18, 44, 45, 60

Ant-Man (Scott Lang) **44–45**

Asgard 20, 21, 59

Avengers' Charter **8–9**

Baron Helmut Zemo 65

Black Order 63

Black Panther 29, **40-43**

Black Widow **30–33**, 34, 35

Blue Marvel 46

Captain America 12, 19, **24–27**, 28, 29, 35

Captain Britain 46

Captain Marvel 48

Captain Universe 47

Doctor Strange **55**

Drax 50, **52**

Falcon **28–29**

Gamora 50, **52**

Grim Reaper 64

Groot 50, **53**

Guardians of the Galaxy **50–53**

Hawkeye 30, 31, **34–35**

Helicarrier 57

Hulk 7, **22-23**, 63

Iron Man 7, 9, **10–13**, 15, 30, 34, 35

Jocasta 47

Kang the Conqueror 64

Korvac 64

Loki 7, 21, **58–59**

Luke Cage 46

Madame Hydra 65

Manifold 49

Mjolnir 20–21

Ms. Marvel 49

Pym Particles 14, 16, 35, 44, 45

Quicksilver 36, 37, **48**

Red Skull 26–27, 28

Rocket Raccoon 50, **52–53**

S.H.I.E.L.D. 32, **56–57**

Scarlet Witch **36–37**

Spectrum 48

Spider-Man **54**

Spider-Woman 47

Star-Lord 50, **51**, 53

Stark Industries 10, 30

Stark Tower 13

Super-Soldier serum 24, 25

Taskmaster 65

Thanos 51, 52, **62–63**

Thor 7, 15, **20–21**, 22, 59

Ultron 15, 19, 37, 38, 39, **60–61**

Vibranium 25, 41

Vision **38–39**, 60

Wakanda 40, 41, 43

Wasp 7, 15 , **16–19**